The House of Governors

A New Idea in American Politics
Aiming to Promote Uniform
Legislation on Vital Questions, to
Conserve States Rights, to Lessen
Centralization, to Secure a Fuller,
Freer Voice of the People, and to
Make a Stronger Nation

by

William George Jordan

British Library Cataloguing-in-Publication Data
A catalogue record for this book is available from the
British Library

William George Jordan

William George Jordan was born on 6 March 1864 in New York City, USA. He took his university education at the *City College of New York* and began his literary career as an editor of *Book Chat* in 1884. After a brief spell (1888-91) editing *Current Literature* - a magazine offering an eclectic combination of literature review and contemporary commentary, Jordan relocated to Chicago. It was here that he first lectured on his system of Mental Training; although not with any great success. In 1897 Jordan moved back to New York and was hired as the managing editor for *The Ladies Home Journal,* after which he moved on to edit *The Saturday Evening Post.* This substantial editing career is not Jordan's best known achievement however – his essays and thoughts on education and 'mental training' have garnered the most attention. In July 1891 *The Chicago Inter-Ocean* printed an interview with Jordan on his 'mental training'. After the article was published he received so many inquiries that he scheduled a long lecture tour on the subject. *The Inter-Ocean* reported that 'during the past few weeks the calls from Chicago have been so numerous, enthusiastic and positive for lecture courses and private society classes that he has concluded to resign his position in New York and come to Chicago.' In 1894, Jordan published a short pamphlet; *Mental Training, A Remedy for Education,* which opened with the following lines; 'here are two great things that education should do for the individual—it should train his senses, and teach him to think. Education, as we know it to-day, does not truly do either; it gives the individual only a vast accumulation of facts, unclassified, undigested, and seen in no true relations. Like seeds kept in a box, they may be retained, but they do not grow.' Jordan's allegorical style was widely utilised in all his works, and he penned his first book, *The Kingship of Self-Control,* in 1898. This was followed by a further nine texts, all on the subject of self-improvement; a theme which he continued writing on for the rest of his life. *The Majesty of Calmness* (1900) was perhaps his most popular self-help book. Despite these successes, Jordan's most influential writing was actually a political tract. In *The House of Governors* (1907), he aimed to 'promote uniform legislation on vital questions, to conserve states' rights, to lessen centralisation, to secure a fuller, freer voice of the people and to make a stronger nation.' The work was circulated to each state governor and to President Theodore Roosevelt, and was incredibly well received. His ideas were put into practice and the first 'meeting of the governors' was held in Washington, on 18 January, 1910 – with Jordan as its secretary. He was dropped as secretary a year later, but nevertheless, this group is a key part of his legacy.

At the age of fifty-eight, Jordan married Nellie Blanche Mitchell, in New York City at the Grace Episcopal Church. The marriage was a happy one, for the short time it lasted, but sadly Jordan died just six years later of pneumonia on 20 April 1928, at his home in New York.

THE HOUSE OF GOVERNORS

HE atmosphere of political thought in the nation today is permeated with restless rebellion of protest against the growing centralization at Washington. Rumblings of revolt in the public press are becoming louder and more unmistakable, and political leaders are furbishing the dingy armor of States rights in preparation for battle. The usurping by the government of the lawmaking power of the States is declared to be a forsaking of the great principle of democracy, the rock upon which the fathers founded the Republic.

The federal government, following the spirit of the age, is itself becoming a trust—a great governing trust, crowding out, and threatening openly still further to crowd out, the States, the small jobbers in legislation. As the wealth of the nation is concentrating in the hands of the few, so is the guidance of the destinies of the American people becoming vested in the firm, tense fingers of a small legislative syndicate. The nation soon will be no longer a solid, impregnable pyramid, standing on the broad, firm, safe base of the united action of a united people, but a pyramid dangerously balanced on its apex—the uncertain wisdom of a few.

There is a growing realization percolating through the varied strata of politics down to the man in the street that the new centralization is a menace. It is a menace. It is not in harmony with the spirit of the constitution, its very essence, though it may be in no technical disaccord with its letter. Had the invasion of the self-governing rights of the States been manifested in evil laws forced into being through a dominated Congress the whole country would have risen to meet the issue at once, but it has come with needed legislation, wise provisions and vital issues, and because of this guise it is all the more dangerous because more insidious. The government of the founders was fraternal; the new government threatens to become paternal.

Were the dictates of any centralized administration inspired with the absolute wisdom of omniscience and executed with the relentless certainty of omnipotence, with every microscopic phase of every act consecrated to the best and highest good of the whole country, it would still be a menace. It is establishing a dangerous precedent—it is placing the self-governing power of the States in pawn with the federal government, with the chances of the ticket becoming lost or the interest rate being raised or some other technicality occurring that might make redemption difficult or even impossible. The mantle of infallibility of one administration may not drop serenely on the shoulders of its successor—wisdom, exalted ideals, and broad, unselfish statesmanship are not always hereditary in office.

This centralization has not been the work of one administration. It has been evolving for years. During the present term it has merely assumed a more vivid, picturesque, startling phase, sufficiently distinct to be portentous, but this centralization is natural and under past conditions inevitable. If there is today federal usurpation of States rights it is so merely because the States have largely abrogated their rights through disuse—through lack of proper exercise. The States themselves have been to blame. Unless they rouse themselves to immediate action the condition may become irremediable, and America will then be but an autocracy under the false guise of a democracy.

Reference to the constitution will show the privileges the people have been, perhaps unconsciously, surrendering. The constitution clearly defines the powers of the federal government in all its branches. The ninth amendment says:— "The enumeration in the constitution of certain rights shall not be construed to deny or disparage others retained by the people." The tenth amendment says:—"The powers not delegated to the United States by the constitution nor prohibited by it to the States are reserved to the States respectively, or to the people." Here was the States' warrant for action, yet corruption and mismanagement had grown brazen, graft flourished, arrogant dominations of trusts became more reckless, illegal aggregations of wealth towered higher in their insolence, bribing of legislators grew more flagrant, patriotism and loyalty were continuously sacrificed on the altar of politics—these and a dozen similar evils, sapping the life of the Republic, were not met by the States when they had the opportunity in their hands.

A few States really did show vitality and virility and earnestly sought to meet the evils, failing to a degree in their efforts by the largeness of their task and the lack of coöperation from their sister States. The situation grew desperate. Then came a federal administration with nerve, courage and resoluteness, and sought seriously to begin to solve the problem—to save the situation.

If the administration went beyond its rights, if it for a time trespassed on States rights, it was because the States were culpably negligent and in-

3

active. If there is a fire smoking in the hold of an ocean steamer and the captain and crew fold their arms in complacent inactivity, hoping the fire will die out, it is the duty of the passengers or any of them to head and organize a bucket corps to stifle the flames. But when it is all over and the captain and crew waken to the realization of their dereliction and learn their lesson they would be foolish to let this emergency corps run the ship. Have the States learned their lesson and awakened to their duty or will they continue to let centralization govern the ship of States?

The trusts for years had been growing more colossal, aggressive and law-defying. The press of the nation chronicled the details, kept hammering at real evils, seeking to rouse legislation. The people talked of it with a sense of abject hopelessness as if an earthquake were coming and they saw no escape. There was unending talk as monotonous as a phonograph with practically as little results. The States as a whole did little or nothing. Then the government passed the Anti-Trust Law, the thin edge of the wedge of broadening legislation.

The iniquitous rebates of the railroads, that forced thousands of small dealers into bankruptcy and restrained commerce and the natural development of individual interests, continued for decades practically, if not actually, untouched by the hand of State law. The States could have met the evil, partially at least, but they did nothing. Then the government passed the rate bill.

Grasping capital, holding nothing sacred, not even the food of babes, carried adulteration and food poisoning to a point where it seemed that the only way to live was to give up eating. The newspapers exposed it, the magazines exploited

4

it, scientists lectured on it, societies were formed to fight it, but the States waited—for the federal government to pass the Pure Food Law.

The President and the Secretary of State have declared repeatedly that the States are not able to unite in the making of laws on questions of national importance and that therefore the power to make these laws must become vested in the federal government. With all due deference, however, may it not be asked whether the failure of the States to make uniform legislation has not been due to the lack of any method of the States to get together in conference as, States? Were this provided wherein is it impossible for the States themselves to handle this legislation? That there are difficulties is self-evident; that these difficulties are insurmountable is open to question. Should not any plan that has within it a germ of hope be tried, if the trying imply no danger to the fullest safety of the Union, before we hopelessly accept as a finality the imputation that the States are no longer fit for self-government? Secretary Root not only says that "these things the States no longer do adequately," but also that "they (the States) are no longer capable of adequately performing." The honorable Secretary conjugates the impotence of the States in the present and the future tense.

There does seem to be one simple, practicable method yet untried which the writer desires here to propose—one that is in such perfect harmony with the letter and the spirit of the constitution that it would require no constitutional amendment; one that might not even require (for an initial trial, at least) legislative action in any State; one that upsets no established order in the conduct of the nation; one that would bring the States into

5

closer unity and harmony without lessening in any degree loyalty and allegiance to the federal government; in short, a plan that if worked out successfully in practice would put the rights of the States on a firm, recognized basis and make centralization forever an impossibility in the American Republic. The plan which I wish here humbly and respectfully to present to the leaders in the political activities of the country, to our Governors and legislators, and to the American press and public is the organization of

THE HOUSE OF GOVERNORS.

It is proposed that the Governors of the forty-five States meet annually for a session of two to three weeks to discuss, consult and confer on vital questions effecting the welfare of the States, the unifying of State laws and the closer unity of the States as a nation. The House of Governors would have no lawmaking power, nor should it ever aspire to such power. Its force would be in initiative, in inspiration and in influence. The Governors would seek to unite on a general basis of action on great questions to be submitted to the legislatures of the respective States in the Governor's messages. It would seem that an august, dignified body of forty-five Governors, representing their States, with the lawmaking power of forty-five legislatures behind them, should in time become an inherent part in the American idea of self-government and a powerful factor for good in the nation.

This brief statement covers the broad lines of the suggestion and for it we ask consideration in connection with the amplification and detail of the thought that follows this outline.

In the Congress of the United States the Senators, chosen as they are by the State legislatures, nominally represent their States, but not the people of their States, for the latter have no direct voice in their selection. The members of the House of Representatives do not represent their States, but simply districts of their States. With ties to their constituents and with duties and obligations to them they may in theory have the interest of the entire State as a matter of paramount importance in their hearts, but in fact they never lose sight of the finality of value in the Congressional district. The Governor of the State, however, is elected by the people, is directly responsible to the people and is in constant touch with the people, keeping his fingers close-pressed on the pulse of their needs and problems. The voice of the Governors, therefore, in the proposed new house means a new, direct, vital representation of the people in the affairs of the State and in the harmony of the States making up the nation such as the people have never yet had in the life of the republic.

On many great questions it is difficult to secure national legislation and on others it is impossible to secure it without constitutional amendment. Today we have no national holiday legalized by Congress for the States—not even the Fourth of July, Thanksgiving Day or Christmas—yet by the action of the separate States these days are universally observed. They are national in scope, but not national in genesis, so if the legislatures of the forty-five States, working together through the House of Governors for uniform laws, should pass the same law the practical effect of a national law would be secured without federal action.

In the House of Governors no majority vote should be binding on the minority. Should even forty-four members of the House in full session agree, the one member not concurring should have absolute freedom of action and he or his successor would probably join the majority side at the next session of the House. The House should determine by vote the ratio of the members present that is to be considered the minimum requisite for the initial impulse for action toward uniform State legislation throughout the country on the specific question. Should the number of votes be below the ratio set as a basis of unity the matter could go over to the next session for reconsideration.

If on the subject of, let us say, divorce, twenty-five members of the House were to agree on a general plan the twenty-five Governors thus concurring would suggest to their respective legislators in their ensuing messages the passage of a bill in accordance with the recommendation. The legislatures, of course, would have absolute freedom to pass it or not as they deemed best, but the recommendation would have a greater dynamic effect and a stronger moral influence when each legislature knows that twenty-four other legislatures are considering the same proposed law. Let us assume that of the twenty-five States eighteen passed this bill, in the other seven were public sentiment sufficiently aroused and the people sufficiently united this question might be made an issue in the next campaign and those legislators elected who would be pledged to carry through the bill.

At the next meeting of the House, with the

prestige of the adoption of the law by eighteen States, ten new converts might be made among the Governors non-concurring in the first session, and so in the course of a few sessions we might have uniform State legislation on this vital problem without federal action. A law thus finally passed by all of the States would more truly represent the sentiment of the American people than any law passed by the federal government, even if constitutional amendment or new revised interpretation of the constitution empowered the passing of the law.

The annual meeting of such an able deliberative body as the House of Governors would receive careful attention from the press of the country. Every State being represented by its Governor, and the problems discussed being vital ones, there would be secured throughout the country simultaneous consideration of the questions before the House, a thorough, practical ventilation of the subjects and a general study of the proposed remedies. Vague diffused public opinion, through the influence of the House of Governors, would be crystallized into public sentiment, and this sentiment, the people's voice, could compel legislation.

The general opinion of the people of this country today, it would seem, is against capital punishment—a sad relic of primitive barbarism still persisting with war in this vaunted twentieth century civilization—yet there is no method today by which this unexpressed public opinion can be vitalized, transmuted into public sentiment manifesting itself in uniform State laws, yet the House of Governors might accomplish it as part of the work of a single session.

The lack of uniformity in State legislation today is so clearly recognized as an evil in our political system that further details in this article seem unnecessary. Any plan that even faintly foreshadows the possibility of bringing order out of this chaos of complexity and contradiction would seem worthy of really serious consideration.

The House of Governors seems to offer no chance for graft, collusion, combination, pairing off, the working of private interests, bribery, jobbery, corruption or any of the other diseases to which legislative bodies are liable. This immunity arises from the non-lawmaking character of the House. It is said to be easier to buy State legislatures than to purchase federal action or federal inactivity. The House would thus have the dignity, character and poise of the federal government. The Governors here would be subject to no pressure, they would not be likely to be carried off their feet by the whirlwind eloquence of one of their members advocating some Utopian scheme or some trust measure masquerading as a plan of public benevolence. But even if temporarily captivated they would probably cool on reflection, and there is no chance of the gold-brick fallacy proposed being able to stand the acid test of wide public discussion by press and people and to pass the safeguarding process of forty-five legislators.

It seems advisable that the meetings of the House of Governors should be annual, though the sessions of State legislators are annual in only six of the States, while quadrennial in one and biennial in thirty-eight. In 1907 only six States have legislative sessions, but in 1908 forty-one States—or all but Alabama, Oregon, Virginia and Wyoming—hold sessions. Were the House of Governors to meet during the present year a splendid test of the value of their session could be made in January, 1908, all the forty-one State Legislatures then meeting, except Florida (April), Louisiana (May), Georgia (June) and Vermont (October).

It may be objected that the Governors could not spare time away from their official duties to attend sessions of the House, but as their bodily presence at home is not necessary, except when the Legislature meets, this objection is more theoretic than real, and the State could for a term of two or three weeks be left to the Lieutenant Governor or to the Secretary of State as Acting Governor.

The place of meeting of the House of Governors should not be in Washington, D. C. (except possibly its first session), but successively in State capitals selected by vote of the House or by the decision of a committee, and giving the honor of the session successively to States in rotation on a general plan of choice, selecting for the first year perhaps an Eastern State, the following year a Western State, then a Northern, then a Southern and last a Central State, repeating the order of choice till the forty-five (Oklahoma, the forty-sixth, not having been officially admitted to the Union at this writing), shall have been recognized.

The date of the session should be at a season that would avoid the time of the sitting of the State Legislatures and the months directly preceding the November elections. The cost of the meetings of the House of Governors should be little more to each State than the traveling and other necessary personal expenses of its Governor for the brief period of the session. Any

State selected for an annual meeting would gladly provide its legislative assembly room for the meetings of the House, with accommodations therein for visitors (perhaps by invitation) and press representatives at the daily sessions. The force of doorkeepers, pages, stenographers and others needed for the brief term should be but a slight tax on the hospitality of the State.

In order that the members of the House of Governors should be fully informed in advance of the topics to be discussed and to save valuable time for the session it is suggested that it shall be the duty of the chairman of the House or of the committee appointed therefor to invite the members, say four months before the session, to send in lists of suggestions of vital topics for consideration. These lists when received from all Governors would be tabulated in the order of their importance and submitted as candidates of topics. The Governors would then mark a given number of subjects, a number in excess of those likely to be covered during the session, and from these lists of preferences returned to the chairman, or committee, the resultant official list of elected subjects would then be sent to each member, thus giving him time for thoughtful preparation for the session, and enable the House to take up its programme of work, with no loss of time, immediately after electing the necessary officers.

Among the subjects of vital interest to the entire country and on which free discussion tending toward uniform legislation is desirable may be named: marriage and divorce, rights of married women, corporations and trusts, insurance, child labor, capital punishment, direct primaries, convict labor, prison reform, contracts, uniform system of conveyancing, inheritance tax, income tax, mortgages, referendum, election reforms and similar topics. The House of Governors might have a consulting board of legal advisers, specialists in constitutional law and federal and State legislation, if such counsel were needed.

On every important question brought before the House it would be found that some one or two States had progressed further than others in some direction. Each State working out its own problem has to a degree specialized, as Oregon with its referendum, by which the people direct their legislators and by which party machines have been abolished. Those States that have partially solved great problems in self-government have valuable material in the form of documents, reports, discussions, blue books, records, etc., giving in concrete form the results of their experiments and experiences which would be inspiring to Governors desiring to look into these questions with the fullest light possible at the psychologic moment of deep personal interest.

We have, annually, conventions of educators, of lawyers, of ministers, of doctors, of scientists and of members of every profession, trade and industry, meeting to become acquainted, to confer on matters of common interest and to strike the fire of new wisdom or inspiration from mutual contact, yet two State Governors may never meet except accidentally or incidentally at some dinner or political gathering. The newspapers report even these meetings only because of the opportunity they afford to spring again on the public a worn-out epigrammatic colloquy between two Southern Governors on the subject of thirst.

The Congress of the United States would in

no wise be disturbed in its normal work as marked out for it by the constitution by the institution of the House of Governors. There need be no conflict between Congress and the new house, for the States, quietly working out their own problems by the 'light of their united wisdom, could not trespass on the specific legislation left by the constitution to the sole and absolute charge of the federal government.

The House of Governors, even if it were merely a meeting-place for the heads of our State governments, would be of value, but with regular conferences on the broad basis of mutual helpfulness in the unifying of our laws and of combined action in staying the insidious invasion of centralized government, with the sympathy and coöperation of the people of the country and with the lawmaking powers of the State legislatures led into harmony, shamed into activity or forced to do the people's will, the House of Governors, it would seem, should become in a few years a mighty force in the American Government. It should give the people greater power, strengthen the States by granting them fuller liberty, unite and unify them more perfectly and make the united States more truly the United States.

We need in our country today less politics and more statesmanship, less party and more patriotism. We need an awakening to higher ideals. We need a higher conception of America's place and destiny in the evolution of the world. We need something nobler as a purpose than our self-satisfied complacency at the material prosperity of the nation, for there is a moral and ethical success that is never rung up on a cash-register. We need the scourging of the money changers out of the temple of legislation—State and national. We need a purifying and ennobling of the body politic. We need the clear clarion voice of a great inspiration to rouse the States to their duty—not the gilded phrases of mere rhetoric, but the honest eloquence of a high and exalted purpose like that ringing speech of Patrick Henry's, a century and a quarter ago, which breathes the very spirit of the present hour of need when it is said that the States are too weak to do their duty and must surrender to government centralization:—

"They tell us that we are weak, unable to cope with so formidable an adversary. But when will we be stronger? Will it be the next week or the next year? Shall we gather strength by irresolution and inaction? Shall we acquire the means of effectual resistance by lying supinely on our backs and hugging the delusive phantom of hope until our enemies shall have bound us hand and foot? Sir, we are not weak if we make a proper use of those means which the God of nature has put into our power."

Whatever tends to lessen the right of the American people to be absolutely self-governing, whatever tends to take from eighty million people their privileges and to hypothecate them in the hands of a few, is a menace in principle, hazardous in what it portends and in what it makes possible.

The plan of the House of Governors is simple, seemingly feasible, cannot possibly do harm and may have within it the germ of great good. Is it not worth a trial?